OUR AMAZING WORLD
SHARKS

Kay de Silva

Aurora

Contents

A Grey Reef Shark swimming serenely in search of food.

SHARKS

Sharks are a type of fish. These fierce warriors of the sea have been around for over 400 million years. This makes them older than dinosaurs.

ANATOMY

Just like other fish, sharks have strong, streamlined bodies. Unlike other fish, sharks' skeletons are not made of bone. They are made of cartilage. Cartilage is tough, yet light and flexible. This enables sharks to be great swimmers.

Sharks also do not have scales. Instead they are covered in spikes. Although sharks look smooth, their bodies feel rough, just like sandpaper.

They have 5 to 7 pairs of gills on the sides of their heads that help them to breathe. Sharks' livers are large, fat, and oily, helping them to keep afloat.

Remora hitching a ride on a Lemon Shark.

HABITAT

Sharks are found in warm waters across the world. Most sharks prefer to live in the *sunlit zone*, which is the top 600 feet (180 meters) of the ocean. This water is warm and flowing. Some sharks such as the *Bull Shark* may live in freshwater.

A lush coral reef in the sunlit zone is the perfect shark habitat.

MIGRATION

Sharks can easily change their habitat. They are known to swim thousands of miles to find food. They also migrate to mate and give birth.

Sharks are cold-blooded. This means that they do not have a constant body temperature. They take on the temperature of the water in which they live, so when it gets too cold for comfort, sharks will migrate to keep warm.

White Tip Sharks swimming across choppy ocean waters.

The ocean's top predator relies on its keen senses.

SENSES

Sharks are said to be far-sighted. They are able to see better from a distance than close-up. Their eyes are sensitive to light. Their pupils open and close as the light changes, just like the pupils of humans. This does not happen in most other fish.

Sharks have excellent hearing. Sharks' ears cannot be seen, as they are inside their heads. They can pick up low frequency sounds and vibrations.

The Ragged Tooth Shark navigating the Aliwal Shoal, South Africa.

ELECTRO-SENSORS

All animals emit electrical signals. Sharks have *electro-sensors* that can pick up these signals. They are more sensitive to electrical signals than any other animal.

These extraordinary senses are useful when hunting. They can detect electrical currents created by the muscles of other fish swimming in the ocean. Some sharks are able to sense tiny pressure changes created by injured fish struggling to swim.

A Sand Tiger showing off its impressive jaws.

JAWS

Sharks have awesome jaws. Their jaws are lined with several rows of teeth. They may have thousands of teeth at a time. These teeth are made of bone.

Sharks lose thousands of teeth during a lifetime. Their teeth wear out or drop off. When sharks lose teeth, other teeth will move up immediately from a back row to replace them. This is why shark teeth may be found washed up on beaches.

A Bull Shark closing in on its prey.

FEEDING

Most sharks are carnivores. This means they eat the flesh of other animals. Their food is called *prey*.

Some sharks eat only plankton and small fish such as anchovies and sardines. These sharks eat a few times every day. Other sharks may choose to prey on bigger animals such as seals and other sharks. These sharks can go for many weeks without food.

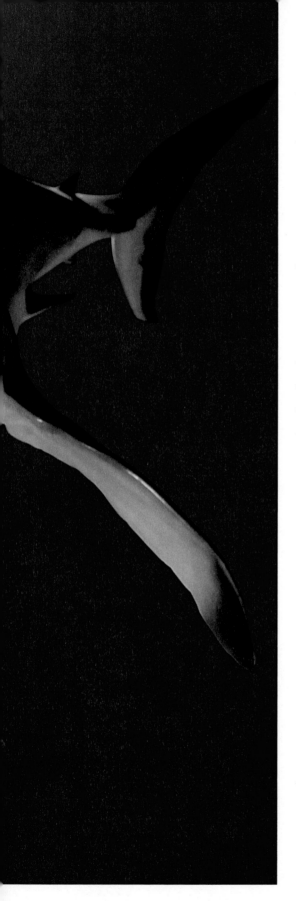

HUNTING

Sharks use their excellent senses to hunt. Their best tool when hunting is their bodies. Sharks have strips of nerves along their bodies called lateral lines. These enable sharks to pick up scents, just like a hunting dog uses its nose. These giant noses can pick up not just the scent, but also the shape of the animal emitting the scent.

Sharks also have the ability to *camouflage* themselves. This means that they can blend in with their environment as they hunt. In this way they remain hidden, ready to pounce when the time is right.

An approaching Great White and a fleeing seal.

SHARK PACKS

Most sharks swim and hunt alone. *Hammerhead Sharks* swim in packs or groups. They sometimes swim in groups of over 100 during the day. At night they hunt for food alone.

A School of Hammerhead Sharks in Galapagos.

A Baby Leopard Shark swimming in a tidal pool.

BABY SHARKS

Baby sharks are called pups. Some sharks hatch from eggs, like birds. Others grow inside their mothers, like humans.

Sharks can have 1 to 100 pups at a time. Shark mothers look for safe places to lay their eggs or give birth. However, they do not care for their pups after they are born.

Black Tip Reef Sharks swimming in tropical waters.

BLACK TIP REEF SHARKS

Black Tip Reef Sharks are found in the warm waters of the Pacific and Atlantic oceans. Clear black markings on their fins make them easy to spot. These sharks are not very large, but are aggressive and fast.

Their favorite prey includes sardines and stingrays. Like dolphins and whales, they, too, are often found *breaching* or leaping out of the water.

BULL SHARKS

Bull Sharks are commonly found on tropical shores. They often travel inland and live in fresh water. Bull Sharks get their name from their short, blunt snout and tubby appearance. They are also known to head-butt their prey before they attack.

Despite their appearance, these sharks are fast and agile. They eat anything they see. This includes dolphins, fish, and other sharks. They also may attack humans who cross their path. For this reason they are known as the world's most dangerous sharks.

A pair of ferocious Bull Sharks on the prowl.

A Scalloped Hammerhead Shark swimming over a coral reef.

HAMMERHEAD SHARKS

Hammerhead Sharks get their name from the shape of their heads. The eyes placed at the ends of their heads allow them to quickly scan their environment. They then use their unusually-shaped heads to pin their prey to the sea floor. They eat with their mouths, which are found underneath their heads.

Stingrays are their favorite meal. They also eat fish, squid, crabs, lobsters, and other sea creatures.

Hammerhead Sharks live in moderate and tropical regions. During summer these sharks travel in packs to cooler waters.

A Great White Shark hunting on the South African coast.

GREAT WHITE SHARKS

Great White Sharks are the largest and most aggressive sharks. Shark pups are about 5 feet (1.5 meters) at birth. Adults grow to be about 3 times as long. They can weigh over 4,500 pounds (2,000 kilograms). Despite their size, adult Great White Sharks can swim up to 45 mph (miles per hour).

Their teeth may measure over 2.5 inches (6.5 centimeters). Young sharks eat other fish, sharks, and rays. Older sharks enjoy sea mammals, including seals and sea lions. When hunting, they surprise their prey by quietly waiting under water and breaching the water to catch their prey.

Great Whites are known to be dangerous to humans. Great White Shark attacks, however, are rare.

Lemon Sharks feeding in the shallow waters of the Bahamas.

LEMON SHARKS

Lemon Sharks are commonly found in the Caribbean. They get their name from their light brown and yellow skin. Their color helps them stay hidden as they rest close to the sandy bottom in shallow waters.

Although these sharks live in shallow areas, they may dive up to 1,300 feet (400 meters) in search of food. Lemon sharks are known to chase their prey. This includes other sharks, large birds, squid, and all types of rays.

A Nurse Shark resting on the ocean floor.

NURSE SHARKS

Nurse Sharks are bottom-dwelling sharks. They are commonly found around the coastal waters of Central America. They live in reefs and channels where food is abundant. These sharks prey on fish, octopuses, shrimp, and stingrays.

Nurse Sharks are *nocturnal animals*. This means that they are not active during the day. They spend the night hunting. They then return to the same spot every morning to rest.

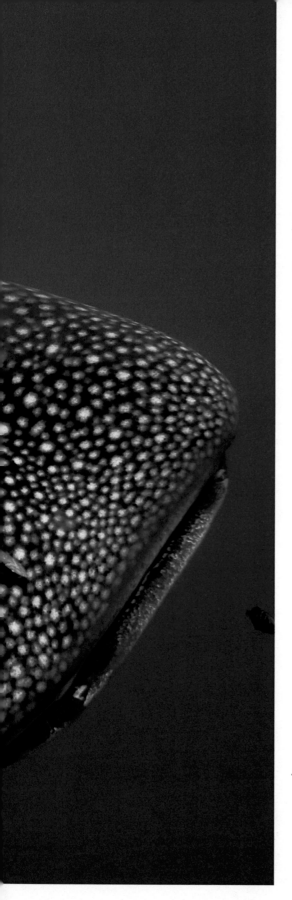

WHALE SHARKS

Whale Sharks are the largest of all fish. Adults can grow to be over 40 feet (12 meters) long. They can grow as large as whales. Like whales, they are *filter feeders*. They use their massive jaws to filter large objects. They swallow only tiny fish and other small sea creatures that cross their paths. Their favorite food is plankton.

Whale Sharks are found in all tropical seas. Despite their size, these sharks are harmless. Divers are known to hitch a ride on their large bodies.

A close encounter with a Whale Shark.

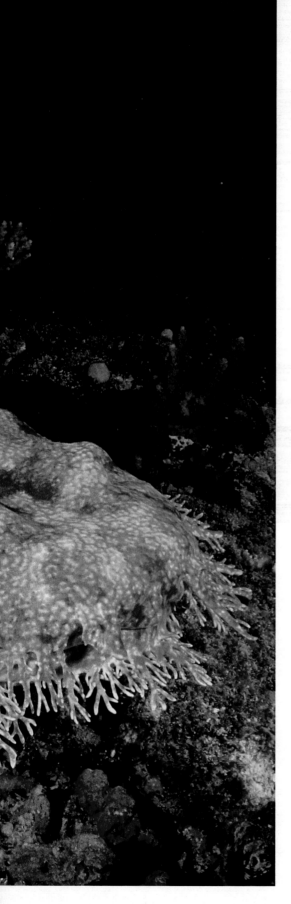

WOBBEGONGS

Wobbegongs are bottom dwelling sharks. They spend most of their time resting on the sea floor. Theses sharks are well camouflaged. Their unusual markings make them look like carpets, so they are also called Carpet Sharks.

Wobbegongs have whisker lobes around their jaws that look like seaweed. They use these lobes to attract and catch small fish.

A Tasselled Wobbegong goes unnoticed on the sandy ocean floor.

ROLE IN THE ECOSYSTEM

Sharks play an important role in keeping ocean life alive. They eat the weak and sick members of the sea. This stops the spread of diseases. They also act as guards to make sure that other animals do not overuse corals and sea beds.

Sharks are the guardians of the ocean's ecosystem.

Shark or man—who is the greater predator?

SHARK ALERT!

Like most animals, sharks attack to defend themselves, if they feel threatened. This usually happens because they are chased, grabbed, speared, or harmed in any other way.

Sharks also like to investigate new objects in their environments. They use their mouths to do this. This is the reason why many people who encounter sharks get away without being seriously injured.

Despite what books and movies may portray, most sharks are not aggressive. Every day millions of people work and play in the sea. Of these people, every year 70 to 100 people are bitten by sharks; only about 10 are killed.

Humans are not part of sharks' regular diet. Every year, however, millions of sharks are killed by humans for food and sport.

OUR AMAZING WORLD

COLLECT THEM ALL

WWW.OURAMAZINGWORLDBOOKS.COM

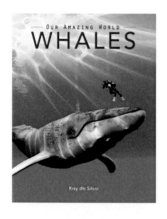

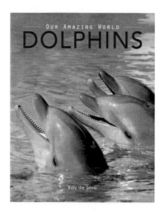

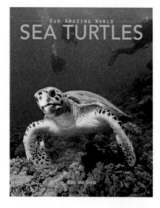

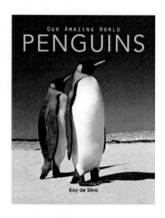

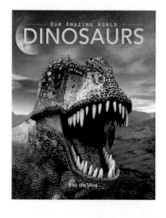

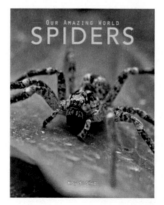

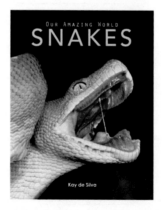

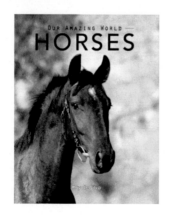

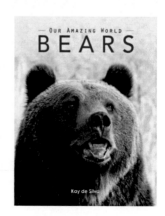

Aurora
An imprint of CKTY Publishing Solutions

www.ouramazingworldbooks.com